Jennifer Lopez on Life, Love, and Show Business

by Toby A. Welch

Cover art by Olivier Chareyre

Jennifer Lopez on Life, Love, and Show Business

Jennifer Lopez is one of the greatest entertainers of all time. She is a triple threat – a successful singer, actress, and dancer. As if that isn't enough, she has conquered television, too. The mother of twins born in 2008, Lopez is just as known for her rollercoaster love life as she is for her phenomenal career.

What follows are quotes spoken by Lopez on all aspects of her life. Each quote is attributed to its original source so you can see it wasn't pulled out of thin air. Hope you enjoy reading the gems that Lopez has shared in the past 20+ years. As a bonus, after the Lopez quotes you'll find a smattering of quotes about the superstar spoken by those in the entertainment industry and those who know her best.

Table of Contents:

LIFE

"Transcendental meditation."

On how she stays young. January 20, 2016. *Las Vegas Sun*

"I mean, the whole idea is that this family is something that is very reflective of our society right now so, yes, me being a single mom, their dad doesn't live at home with them. They have three stepbrothers from two other moms, you know, that's not traditional."

On having a non-traditional family. May 29, 2013. *ABC News*

"It's something that we just started and we just formed. It's something we thought about for a long time, to form a foundation where we could help women and children around the world in different areas, including health care and education. And right now, our focus is on telemedicine."

On setting up a charitable foundation, Maribel Foundation, a non-profit Lopez established with her sister, Lynda, to encourage better health care options for women and children. June 16, 2010. *CNN*

"I liked my upbringing there and it gave me incentive. Just the street smarts and the savvy."

On being born and bred in the Bronx. January 22, 2016. *The Independent*

"I don't drink. Don't like the taste. It would be a waste of money. Never done drugs either."

On her clean-living lifestyle. January 22, 2016. *The Independent*

"It is a little bit insane. I take it one day at a time. Me and the kids are like gypsies. We're traveling all over the place, just getting it done, doing the best we can."

On her schedule and life being full. March 2, 2017. *Today*

"My mother said I could do anything with my life, I could even be President of the United States."

On her mother being her biggest supporter. January 22, 2016. *The Independent*

"As a kid, I would hear the grown-ups talking in the next room, and I wanted to find out what they were doing and then do it. I always had a fear of missing out."

On where she gets her stamina. April 13, 2016. *W Magazine*

"That song *Lay Me Down*? I really, really love it."

On her favorite thing to listen to these days, ballads by Sam Smith. January 22, 2016. *The Independent*

"I would be a painter. I can't paint. But I feel I could learn anything if I worked hard enough. Never say never!"

On what she would do if she wasn't in show business. April 13, 2016. *W Magazine*

"Surrounded by my kids and family on my mother's couch. That's when I feel myself again. That's when I really remember who I am."

On when she feels the most complete. June 19, 2013. *The Telegraph*

"They just made my life so much better. I'm forever grateful that ... you know, I didn't have kids until later and so I almost thought that it wasn't going to happen for me, so I'm very aware that I was blessed with that. It could have been something different. I don't take it for granted one day."

On being 38 when she and then-husband Marc Anthony started their family by having twins. March 2, 2017. *Today*

"Not anytime soon."

On whether she plans to get married again. May 29, 2013. *ABC News*

"I take it one day at a time — I have a lot of help. I don't claim to be Superwoman and do it all by myself."

On juggling work and motherhood and having a life. January 19, 2017. *People magazine*

"When I first got to Hollywood it was like everyone was a size 0 to 4, and I was an 8. These days I'm more of a 6 (she did a triathlon six months after the twins were born). But I never really thought about my looks until [I was] faced with [my] image and people were talking about it. In the beginning, it was always more about just being a good actress."

On her mother teaching her and her two sisters to be confident, to not diet, and to be proud of their bodies. August 4, 2011. *Vanity Fair*

"By nature I am not tough, believe it or not. I am a lover. And with my kids I am even softer. I realize with my son, I have to sometimes be tough, especially now when he's pushing boundaries. With my daughter, I can get a little stern with her and she pretty much will listen. But my son will just scream and yell and run. I'm like, *Aaaaah,* what do I do with this?!"

On needing to deliver tough love with her twins sometimes. March 15, 2012. *Vogue Magazine*

"I wouldn't tell her anything! I'd let her figure it out on her own. Learning from your mistakes shapes who you are. With all the ups and downs you become a richer, more soulful human being. You become more compassionate as you grow."

On what she would tell her 21-year-old self. July 14, 2012. *Stylist magazine*

"I've never tried to hide the fact that I'm Latina. I think that's why Hispanics are like 'She's ours; she's out there, but she belongs to us' and that's true. With the Latino community, I *am* theirs. I *do* belong to them – that's who I am."

On being Latina. April 25, 2006. *People en Español magazine*

"You know, I push myself and I push myself, and every once in awhile, I hit a wall, I get burned out, I get tired, I need a few days off, but on the most part, for the most part, I love what I do. So I push myself, you know? I do. It is part of who I am. So I really think for me right now, it's about finding a balance and kind of taking care of myself and doing what I love and not going overboard."

On staying in shape. May 17, 2017. *ABC News*

"Honestly, I'm not going to make a judgment on it because I don't have to yet. I mean, I'd like to think I'll feel great about myself and age gracefully, but then I think, 'Well, what if I do want a little bit of something?' I'm open to being open."

On plastic surgery. October 31, 2011. *Glamour magazine*

"Just staying at home with the kids and letting them run around, spending normal time with them - you know, not having to go anywhere or do anything because we're always kind of on the run.

I know it's a lot for them. They handle it very well, but I told them just now on the way here, 'Guess where we're going tomorrow?' And they're like, 'Where?' I said, 'We're going home!' They got these big smiles on their faces - they can't wait. Just like me."

On what she does on her days off. December 6, 2013. *Elle Canada*

"I feel like women are knocking those preconceptions down every single day. Every major actress right now is in her forties. The new crop hasn't really come up in the same way, and it's the same with recording artists, too. In old Hollywood, by the time you were 28 you were over; it was so youth-driven. Now people realise how much better women get with experience and wisdom. It's a very 'woman' moment."

On refusing to cave to the notions of how a woman in her 40s should behave. June 19, 2013. *The Telegraph*

"I don't regret what I've been through. I've had ups and downs, super highs and some really low lows. I've been so blessed that I could never say, 'I wish this didn't happen.' It's part of who I am. There's nothing in my life that's so *ugh*. Yes, there are some things that I'm like, *Eww*, but not where I'm worried about [Max and Emme] finding out. I'll tell them myself. No secrets from them."

On whether she wishes some parts of her past weren't so public. August 2, 2010. *Glamour magazine*

"I never took sun when I was younger. I wasn't a drinker, I didn't smoke. But I feel like at the core, it's like how you feel inside and who you are inside kind of shows on your face. And I always used to hear this saying, until you're about 25 or 30, you get the face God gave you. After that, you get the face you deserve. And I always kind of thought, well I better be nice."

On her beauty secret, playing nice. January 5, 2016. *Today*

"Not really. You know, just like anybody else, there are days I feel great when I wake up, and then there are days when I feel more tired or not ready to face the day. To be quite honest, on those days, I really try to think positively.

I try to do a lot of affirmations for good health and positive thinking to just get my mind and my spirit in the right place so I can face whatever it is that I need to face. I remind myself how lucky I am, how fortunate I am to have my children, for all of us to be healthy and to have the life that I have. And to be able to do what I love. And then I try to just go from there."

On whether she ever wakes up feeling unattractive and having a bad day. December 6, 2013. *Elle Canada*

"I think the world is fascinated with Latin culture because we have a certain passion that just doesn't exist in other cultures. It has to do with the beat and the rhythm inside of us; it's just different than anywhere else in the world. When people hear our music, they hear the soundtrack of who we are and it just fills me in a way that no other music does."

On the Latin community and culture. April 25, 2006. *People en Español magazine*

"Even though my life has changed and the circumstances of my life have changed, I still feel very motivated by the same things, which is to make great art and great music and to do good movies and to create things from nothing."

On whether her motivations are the same now as when she first started out. July 14, 2012. *Stylist magazine*

"Motherhood is my first and most favourite thing. It's also the scariest thing, so terrifying and daunting. But it brings me so much joy. I think about being a performer and having all these amazing moments on stage and movie sets. Still nothing matches the joy I get from coming off stage and having my kids waiting there in the wings. That's when my two worlds collide and I feel whole."

On motherhood. June 19, 2013. *The Telegraph*

"I don't mind it! It's not a negative thing. If somebody tells me I look nice, just like any other woman, I love it."

On whether it gets tiresome that people constantly comment on how beautiful she is. March 15, 2012. *Vogue Magazine*

"Marc doesn't cook, but he will prepare an occasional turkey. I like to cook Puerto Rican food. That's what I grew up on: rice, beans, meat, some Italian-American food. I know my way around the kitchen. We enjoy having that normalcy, because we don't have that much of it. We really are a traveling gypsy family."

On whether she and Marc like to cook. August 2, 2010. *Glamour magazine*

"I'm very happy right now. I feel so fortunate. The kids are doing great - they're in school and they're thriving. That makes me the happiest of all. Mommy gets to be creative and I'm home to them every night, so it's all good."

On her life these days. January 20, 2017. *The Brampton Guardian*

"I do have trouble saying no. It's hard for me not to imagine doing everything I am asked to do. Even if I hear a song that someone else has done or watch a film that someone else is in, I think, 'Oh, I would do it like this.' Or, 'I wish I could do it like that.' Luckily, I love to work."

On whether her nonstop pace is ever overwhelming for her.
April 13, 2016. *W Magazine*

"Once you have kids, it's a whole different world. You go along as an actress or performer in this business and it's [always] 'Me, me, me. My business, my career, my things. What am I going to do next?'

When you have kids it becomes not about you, it becomes about them and what's going to make them happy and what's going to make them better, and what's going to be better for them."

On everything she does being for her children. January 20, 2017. *The Brampton Guardian*

"I read something in the Bible, because I read the Bible a lot, and it has to do with perseverance. I don't remember everything in the Bible but this quote said, 'Be happy for your trials because with your trials your faith is tested and when your faith is tested you gain perseverance and when your perseverance is perfect you lack nothing.' And that is the thing: just keep going. That's what I would say to everybody, that's what it's about. You just keep going."

On what is next in her life. April 25, 2006. *People en Español magazine*

"The things I liked when I was, like, 16 and in the Bronx—jeans, cut-up T-shirts—I still like. But I've been exposed to so much now from traveling the world and seeing couture clothes. I used all of that when I created my new line for Kohl's. My style has come from everything, from where I started to where I am today."

On how her style has evolved through the years. October 31, 2011. *Glamour magazine*

"Not only is she the most experienced person for this job and she knows this country — she's lived it on so many different sides already. I live upstairs from her [daughter.] I get to see how often she comes to see her daughter, how often she comes to visit her grandchildren… They're a good, decent, working family who knows this office and I just feel like we will be in amazing hands."

On why she publicly supported Hillary Clinton during the 2016 presidential run. October 31, 2016. *Extra*

"I want to teach him respect and appreciation for women by *being* a great woman."

On what she will teach her son, Max, about love and how to treat women. August 2, 2010. *Glamour magazine*

"I was talking about it with one of my girlfriends — the day our daughters come to us at 19 years old saying, 'I want to get married.' And we know for damn sure that that's not a good idea. Sometimes [Emme] is going to make mistakes, and she's going to have to live through that, just like I did. I know my mother suffered with me through many things. I'm just going to be suffering on the sidelines."

On what she will teach her daughter, Emme, about love. August 2, 2010. *Glamour magazine*

"I'm a hopeless romantic and passionate person when it comes to love. [And] it's not that I didn't love myself before. Sometimes we don't realize that we are compromising ourselves. To understand that a person is not good for you, or that that person is not treating you in the right way, or that he is not doing the right thing for himself — if I stay, then I am not doing the right thing for me. I love myself enough to walk away from that now.

As women, we are naturally giving and we take care of others. I love that part of us and I love doing it. We just have this tendency to put ourselves on the back burner. But we need to be conscious about loving and taking care of ourselves, too. The babies had something to do with this. Because when you feel that love for the first time, it's so selfless and pure that it makes you question … all the ways you acted and were treated…. I'm on a journey to discovering me. So I can teach my babies to do the same thing. So they are always okay, with or without someone."

On the importance of loving yourself first before you can properly love someone else. August 4, 2011. *Vanity Fair*

"Absolutely. I do. But there's no way I can control that. I can only speak for myself and hope that people hear my words, that they see me on television speaking for myself, and hopefully they make their own judgments. At the end of the day, I just hope my work will speak for itself."

On whether she ever feels misunderstood. January 22, 2001. *The Times-Colonist*

"It's fun all the time. It's a wonderful thing but just like anything, it's life. It's real. I'm human, and things, you know, there's ups and downs, but it makes the ups so much better."

On enjoying her life these days and not planning on slowing down. May 17, 2017. *ABC News*

"It was all about Madonna for me. She inspired me to want to sing, to dance, to work hard. I saw those pictures of her running in the park, training, and I thought, 'That's what I need to be doing.' I'm a girl living in the Bronx at this point. I've never seen the inside of a gym, but I thought, 'I'm going to find myself a track.' It wasn't a moment on stage that did it, it was a picture of Madonna in the park."

On who inspired her when she was a young girl. October 21, 2015. *Huffington Post UK*

"My cousins help me, my best friend. It takes a village — you do really learn what that means once you have kids. But I like to wake up with them, I like to put them to bed, and even if I have to go back to work after I spend that couple of hours with them between dinner and when they go to bed, I'll do that."

On using family members and close friends to help raise her twins instead of nannies. October 31, 2011. *Glamour magazine*

"Your whole [life] changes and it's this beautiful, freeing kind of loving feeling.

Things get, in a way, easier, because you know what's important. But also harder, because you just don't want to ever fail them."

On being afraid of failing her children. January 20, 2017. *The Brampton Guardian*

"I think I'm like every woman. I have days when I think I look great and days when I think I look c_ _ _. But when you have kids, it's just about pressing on, no matter how you feel."

On what she sees when she looks in the mirror. June 19, 2013.
The Telegraph

"I'm used to people saying I am sexy. It's always been the way. I am a typical Latino girl. I have curves, I have hips, I have boobs and I have a big bottom. Men have always loved that look.

I developed early. I'd be coming home from school and I'd see men turning to look at me. I was just a kid, about 11, so I had no idea what was going through their minds. My mother was very aware of the effect I had on men. She was terrified I would get pregnant really young. Of course, I hadn't thought of such a thing."

On her sex appeal. June 18, 1999. *The Mirror*

"I thought I was so the tough girl from the Bronx. Like, had it all together. I had this confidence in what I could do. I didn't have so much confidence in who I was and what I had to offer just as a girl."

On having low self-esteem in her 20s. November 4, 2014.
Today

"I'm not a big fan of chunky heels or any shoes that feel and look heavy. I love sleek, refined, and feminine, with a bit of sparkle."

On her favorite kinds of shoes. January 25, 2017. *Vogue Magazine*

"Absolutely. At this point I've been doing it a long time, but sometimes when I do something new, it can be overwhelming.

I feel like people get scared of those feelings, but I don't think you should be scared of being overwhelmed. It's a natural feeling. Just feel it and be like, 'Wow, this is amazing. It doesn't happen every day.' It's exciting."

On whether she ever wakes up wondering how everything in her life has happened. December 6, 2013. *Elle Canada*

"I think of the day my kids were born ... It was in the middle of a snowstorm, and I wore this big white fur coat. I was huge, and it was the only coat that would fit me.

It takes you back to that period in your life. I do the same thing with my closet. I walk in and I see a hat or a pair of shoes or a coat, and I go, 'Wow! I remember I was wearing that the day this happened, or I was walking down the street; or I heard this or my mom said that, or my boyfriend ...' You know what I mean?"

On what she wore when she gave birth to her twins. November 17, 2016. *The Brampton Guardian*

"No. I think one of the reasons that the price went so high is that we didn't want to do it for so long. We weren't into it. I was like, no, I don't really want to. No. No way. But then it got to the point that you go, well, now you're being stupid with these offers... I thought I can set them up. I can put this away just for them."

On whether she had any qualms about selling baby pictures of her twins to *People* magazine for $6 million. October 6, 2008. *The Daily Beast*

"I don't have one person who I can trust most in the world. You have different friends for different things and you want to believe that you can trust all of them."

On whom she trusts most in this world. July 14, 2012. *Stylist magazine*

"There are many [things] that I can't do. Let's not talk about that. Let's talk about the things I can do!"

On what she can't do. January 20, 2017. *The Brampton Guardian*

"I think I realised they were as important – if not more important – when I divorced Marc. I just realised that I had been through that a couple of times and there they still were. Like they say, men come and go, but my girlfriends are always there for me."

On her girlfriends being the thing that kept her going during the tough times after her third divorce. November 11, 2015. *Marie Claire*

"I remember when I had baby fat and my thighs were so out of proportion to my ankles. Then I remember dropping weight and being quite thin. Then, when I got pregnant, I remember watching my back, belly and butt grow and thinking, 'I will never be the same again.' Then I remember right after the twins were born having that weird jiggly belly – and kind of loving that, too. Because I earned that jiggly belly. Then came trying to get my body back into shape and how long that took. A whole year."

On loving her body. June 19, 2013. *The Telegraph*

"I was passionate about what I was doing and in making sure I was right. I think I'm more of a perfectionist now than ever. In my personal life, I'm the most laid-back person, but when it comes to my work, I'm a total perfectionist."

On her tendency to be a perfectionist. January 22, 2001. *The Times-Colonist*

"You have your finger on the pulse, but is it as important? It's funny, I hate the news, the news is so depressing. When I was younger one of my boyfriends used to call me 'The Pretty in Pink Girl' as I kind of like pretty-in-pink movies, I don't like horror movies, I don't like scary or dark or thriller ones. I just want to be happy and that's how I want to believe the world is."

On whether her perspective changed when she became a mother. July 14, 2012. *Stylist magazine*

"I don't get nervous. I don't get depressed. Blah blah blah. There was a time when I was very overworked and I was doing music and movies and so many things. I was suffering from a lack of sleep. And I did have a kind of nervous breakdown. I froze up on a set. Well, not on a set, but in my trailer. I was like - I don't want to move. I don't want to talk. I don't want to do anything. It was on that movie *Enough*. I had a nervous breakdown.

There were no signs leading up to it. You really don't know what's happening at first. I was going, what's going on? It was about five in the afternoon in my trailer and I just sat there. I remember telling my assistant at the time - Arlene - to go get the director Michael Apted and I asked if I could go home because I was feeling so sick and weird. I kept saying, 'I'm not weak. I'm not weak.' It's funny what tricks your mind plays on you. I just didn't want people to think I was falling apart. But when I look back on it now it's so odd to me that those are the words I chose to say: I AM NOT WEAK. Michael let me off and when he left I just sat there and started crying and felt frozen. I didn't want to move. My bodyguard who had been with me for many years picked me up and put me in the car and they took me to a doctor ... Right away they want to give you pills. But I have never liked the idea of pills and kept saying no to that and just kept asking what was wrong with me. 'I'll tell you what's wrong,' the doctor said. 'You're sleep deprived. You're overworked. Go home and go to bed.' He told me to go back to work on Monday after a weekend of sleeping because if I waited longer that I would only get more panicked about working. So that's what I did. I've still never been to a shrink. I'm not a shrinky person."

On her nervous breakdown. October 6, 2008. *The Daily Beast*

"I have the 'stardom glow.' See, I grew up watching real movie stars - Ava Gardner, Rita Hayworth, Marilyn Monroe. Glamorous women like those are why I wanted to get into the business. And from the time I first started off as an actress, each day I had an audition, I'd wake up, do my hair and my makeup, look at myself in the mirror and say, 'I have the stardom glow today.' A lot of people go into meetings and auditions all nervous. No! You've got to have WOW! I tell my actress friends this all the time. I walk into auditions going, 'What's gonna make me different from all the other girls here?' They're looking for the next star to walk into that room. It's about being alive, open, electric, confident. That's the wow."

On her belief that you have nothing to fear but fear itself. February 1, 1998. *Movieline*

"I don't like to talk much about politics because I always feel that when celebrities start talking about politics it gets very weird, but you know, just like anybody else, any other person who has a family that they love, you're like 'Oh, my God, what's going on here?' I don't know when all of this is going to stop and when are things going to change and are we going to look back on this period in time and be like 'God, we really messed up?' I just don't want that to happen, but it feels like it's happening right now."

On what is happening in the world these days. April 25, 2006. *People en Español magazine*

"Marc actually loves Chinese a little *too* much. He'll say, 'I'm really in the mood for Chinese.' I'm like, '*Again?*' "

On whether Chinese takeout really is a staple in her home. August 2, 2010. *Glamour magazine*

"I'm nervous about it, I'll be honest. It's soul-baring."

On how she feels about her book, *True Love*, hitting store shelves. June 12, 2014. *Los Angeles Times*

"Many people have told me it has, and that's something I'm proud of. I was just so infuriated that somebody said you couldn't have a little extra meat on you — because I was by no means fat! That was so mean and closed-minded. I was like, 'No, this is who I am, and this is the type of woman that I grew up with, and it was beautiful and there's no reason to be anybody but myself.' "

On once having a fired a manager who told her to lose weight and whether her attitude of 'I'm happy being curvy' has had an impact on girls. October 31, 2011. *Glamour magazine*

"From my dad I got the calmness necessary to handle this sort of lifestyle. The combination has served me pretty well over the years."

On what her father taught her (Lopez credits her mom for keeping her on the straight and narrow and for her strength.) June 19, 2013. *The Telegraph*

"People kept prepping me for it, but it didn't happen. At the tenth day after giving birth all that chemical stuff did peak - that hormone thing - and I did cry a lot that day because I was having so much trouble moving. I had a c-section. I told them I didn't want to know anything, but afterwards they told me they had cut six layers. That's why you can't walk afterwards. I couldn't get up fast enough to feed the babies. It went on for about three days. Marc was helping out a lot and I was crying and crying and going, 'Oh, Papi … they're going to know everybody more than me. They're going to love everybody more than me!' "

On whether she suffered any postpartum depression. October 6, 2008. *The Daily Beast*

"I didn't experience doubt until later in my life. When I was young, I was just about hard work. But as I got older, I did experience anxiety, doubt, judgment, and it's so easy to lose yourself for a second. I always joke about letting the haters motivate you. *Everybody* has that in their life, people who doubt them or make them feel less than they are. It just takes faith and belief in yourself, and you've got to dig deep into that. That has to come from you — nobody's going to give you that. You can have a great mentor, a great partner, a great love in your life who gives you confidence and makes you feel great about yourself. And that's all wonderful, but at the end of the day, if you don't believe it, all of that means nothing."

On coping with self-doubt. August 2, 2010. *Glamour magazine*

"Are you kidding me? You did not just ask me that."

Lopez's response when Billy Bush asked her, "People have raved about it for years - how do you feel about your butt?" October 12, 2016. *Vivala*

"It's funny the way people come at [Scientology]. To me it's so strange. These are some of the best people I've ever met in my life. You know, they're just lovely, genuine people. The way they ask is such a, 'Uh, are you [a Scientologist]?' It's such a negative thing and I just don't see it that way. My dad has been a Scientologist for 20 years. He's the best man that I know in my life and so, it's weird to me that people want to paint it in a negative way."

On Scientology. November 13, 2015. *Fusion*

"Feminist?! I don't even know what that means any more. It feels like such a Sixties word. Isn't everybody? I don't know, I am a very girly girl, I have a lot of girly friends and I cherish my time with them. They help me through everything. You think about relationships and people going in and out of your life but the women in your life are always there."

On whether or not she is a feminist. July 14, 2012. *Stylist magazine*

"Yeah. I wouldn't mind. Not at all. Because I know that the technologies that they have are very helpful… It's all about communication. That's the thing I really don't like about talking about this. I do know so many great people who do do it, who choose it as a lifestyle and really follow it and it is their religion…I just wish that people wouldn't judge it without knowing what it is."

On whether she would ever consider sending Emme and Max to a Scientology school. October 6, 2008. *The Daily Beast*

"In my mind I first felt like, 'Oh, I'll be back to work right after the babies are born.' But then you don't want to. Even now, it's very difficult for me to leave them in the morning. It just tortures me. I'm like, 'It's been hours; are they wondering where I am? Do they know that I love them so much and I'm thinking only about them?' "

On whether she planned to spend two years at home after her twins were born. August 2, 2010. *Glamour magazine*

"Emme is learning to sew and she's super into it... She makes something every time she goes to this class, and she made a cat costume and so that's what she's wearing. [Max was going as Bowser from Super Mario Bros.]"

On what her twins are going to be for Halloween. October 31, 2016. *Extra*

"I would have to say the women who raised me: my mother and my grandmother. They were very powerful, very strong Puerto Rican women. And they taught me everything I know about working hard, being proper and being a lady."

On who she considers to be the most powerful women in the world. December 6, 2013. *Elle Canada*

"I think a lot of people just don't understand what I'm about. They see me laughing, having a good time and they may think 'Oh, she's so ambitious and everything,' but the thing is that I'm just a creative person. If I could describe myself to somebody that's how I would do it; I'd say 'I'm creative and that's what drives me.' I think people think I'm driven by the money things and all that stuff. They get it so mixed up that they forget that's not why I started doing it. I started doing it because I love to perform."

On who Jennifer Lopez is. April 25, 2006. *People en Español magazine*

"It's my first job to … make sure that's okay or else I couldn't do all the other things I do."

On making the happiness of her children her #1 priority. March 31, 2016. *People magazine*

"They do something to you where you want to do everything right for them. And obviously no parent does everything right. It's this weird thing that happens where you are striving to be as good as you can be so that they turn out well. And that requires that you be a really great, evolved, aware person in every moment. Which is pretty awesome. But it's also putting tremendous pressure on yourself — which is why women feel so guilty!"

On her twins and the perspective they bring to her life. March 15, 2012. *Vogue Magazine*

"I hope I'm teaching them about life by example. Like that with hard work you can accomplish anything; that you have to be charitable; that you have to treat people the way you want them to treat you.

You can tell kids things until you're blue in the face, like 'Don't drink!' But if you drink all day, they're going to probably wind up drinking. They will pick up on that. I just try to be a good mom and set a good example."

On what she hopes she is teaching her twins every day about life. December 6, 2013. *Elle Canada*

"Oh my God, my girlfriends are everything to me. They celebrate with you, they cry with you, they hold you when you need to be held. They laugh with you. They're mean with you! They're always there, and it's just a priceless thing to have."

On whether she has many close women friends. October 31, 2011. *Glamour magazine*

"I know everybody feels this way about their kids, but I just feel like they're super special. I can't wait to see what they do, and I feel like my job is to not mess them up too much. It's unconditional love. I'm trying to stay close to Emme so she feels like she can say anything to me. I remember having that separation from my mom, becoming a teenager and feeling like she didn't understand me. It happens to everybody, but I don't want to think about it! With Emme I feel like learning to take care of her and her emotions teaches me how to take care of myself. Having kids made me understand men better too. Having twins and seeing how Max handles things differently than Emme even though they're at the same level of development, same age and have the same family. Guys just think different! I kept thinking they think like me! But they don't. All those crazy insights are like light bulbs going off in your head with them.

On Friday nights we'll do a sleepover, and we'll watch a movie together in my bed and they'll stay up until around 9:30. They get in sleeping bags on the floor. They are doing really great."

On there being nothing more important in her life than being a mom. February 2, 2015. *People magazine*

"I guess I see something in them that I'd love to become."

On admiring in-control women such as Rita Moreno and Barbra Streisand, who have succeeded in more than one medium. August 5, 2000. *The Spectator*

"We actually had a dinner for her here at the house. It was so inspirational what she accomplished. My mom and sister were in Atlantic City with us on the [day she was confirmed]. Marc was still in bed, and he goes, 'It's happening. She's on the TV. She's getting sworn in.' And she was standing there with her mom. I will never forget this moment: We all stopped and looked, and we all started crying. You just felt it. It was such a huge accomplishment to be the first Latina, to be from the Bronx, to be everything that she is. So we thought we had to do something nice and invited her over. And I told her, 'Just know that you make me want to be better. You make people realize that with hard work, living a good life, you can do anything. You *will* be rewarded for that.' "

On the confirmation of Latina Sonia Sotomayor to the Supreme Court. August 2, 2010. *Glamour magazine*

"More personal stuff stresses me out. I do a lot of praying. You know, I went to 12 years of Catholic school! I'm also very into positive thinking. The minute I feel nervousness or anxiety or fear, I go, 'No, no, that's not a thought that I need to have right now. Everything's great, everything's good, you're going to be fine.' "

On what stresses her out and how she copes with it. October 31, 2011. *Glamour magazine*

"I would if I didn't have to swim in the ocean. That really scared me! If it were in a pool, I'd do it again in a minute. It's an amazing thing to push yourself and to accomplish a goal like that."

On whether she would do another triathlon. August 2, 2010. *Glamour magazine*

"I just think when it's easy, it's great. But when something bad happens is when you really learn. It causes self-examination, it causes you to take a look at yourself. You naturally start analyzing. It's not that you're wrong; it's that sometimes you just need to make adjustments. Change your way of thinking, change your way of doing, change your way of *choosing*."

On what she has learned from her failures. October 31, 2011. *Glamour magazine*

"Don't expect anybody to hand you anything. We have to work for everything in this life. It's one thing to sit back and say 'There's not this and there's not that for us'. If I would've said that, I wouldn't have gotten to where I've gotten. Because it's true, a lot of those things are true. But be creative; do it yourself. Make it happen; write it, go to school. We need writers. My company, Nuyorican Productions, is all about that. We want to employ Latino actors, we want to employ Latino directors, we want to hire writers who know that world as a Latino writer; that's important to me and that's important to my husband, too."

On being a role model for millions of young women. April 25, 2006. *People en Español magazine*

"You really have to learn to not put importance in it. That means the good stuff, as well as the bad stuff. The bad stuff is always tough for your family to deal with. ... But, the good stuff, too. You can't buy into that, either. And just knowing you're going to be judged for everything you do or what you wear or how you are. ... It's just like anybody else. There are some days when you don't feel like it. There are days that you're tired, you know what I mean? And there's days that everybody on the crew you're working with is tired, too.

It's okay for them to be like, 'Ugh!' It's not okay for us to be like that, so it's kind of weird for the actors because everybody's looking at them, you know. You can't just blend into the background and be like, 'I'm not feeling you today' and it's okay. It's a different standard. We're held to a different standard."

On the media weighing in on every aspect of her life. April 25, 2002. *Puerto Rico Herald*

"I feel if in your *mind* you can do it, you can do it. You cannot doubt yourself. Doubt is a killer. You just have to know who you are and what you stand for."

On whether she pushes herself to accomplish things in her life. August 2, 2010. *Glamour magazine*

"I've lived my life and tried to grow and tried to get better in the past few years, really markedly made an effort on that and it shows. It's the fruits of your labor of trying to be a good person and trying to do the right thing and continuing to grow as an artist, as a human being. It proves to me that it works, and that's what I'm going to continue to do."

On her life. March 31, 2016. *People magazine*

LOVE

"Someone can add to your happiness but that's not what's going to make you happy. And I had to get happy on my own. It's been a learning curve. I've had some great loves and I'm sure I'll have more."

On her well known struggles with finding lasting love. January 5, 2016. *Today*

"I think that question is too personal."

On whether she uses handcuffs in the bedroom. April 13, 2016. *W Magazine*

"Marriage is tough. It's not going to be perfect and it's not going to be awful if you're going to stay in it. It's definitely challenging."

On marriage. August 4, 2011. *Vanity Fair*

"Dancers! Musicians are too self-absorbed. They are too concerned with themselves to be great in bed."

On who are better lovers, dancers or musicians. April 13, 2016. *W Magazine*

"It wasn't a great time in my life. It was scary. And we broke up many times before that, and got back together and broke up again, and nobody knew about it. It was very tempestuous.

Towards the end it was emotionally exhausting. It was good that I was young."

On her time with Sean "Puffy" Combs, with whom she was romantically involved for two years, from 1998 to 2000. August 4, 2011. *Vanity Fair*

"I hung in there for seven years. I knew very quickly that it wasn't the right thing."

On her marriage to Marc Anthony. April 13, 2016. *W Magazine*

"When my marriage ended, it was not easy to find forgiveness. It wasn't the dream that I had hoped for, and it would have been easier to fan the flames of resentment, disappointment, and anger. But Marc is the father of my children and that's never going away. So, I have to work to make things right. And that is, by far, the hardest work I do."

On her split with third husband Marc Anthony. April 13, 2016. *W Magazine*

"It was probably my first big heartbreak, and to have one of my best friends, who I'd known for years, who I actually love and did have chemistry with, come into my life and say, 'I'm here.' ... What you need to know is, nobody can save you or heal you. Only you can do that for you."

On Marc Anthony moving into the picture romantically once Lopez split up with Ben Affleck. November 4, 2014. *Today*

"Honesty is really important. I'm looking for someone who is like-minded and respectful, conscious of someone else's feelings and loves themselves enough to have a healthy relationship; someone who will allow me to be myself 100 percent completely and will love me for that person. I don't care [if they're famous]. I think they should have their own life, because the world I have around me can be overwhelming. Bringing someone into the kids' lives is going to be a huge deal. I think, 'Are you good enough for my kids? Are you loving enough? Are you kind enough?' "

On what is important to her in a romantic relationship. February 2, 2015. *People magazine*

"First of all, stop! I don't date younger men. I don't think men have to be younger. It's not about that. I just meet people, and if I go out with them, I go out with them, And if I like them, I like them, and if I don't, I don't. It's about the person, you know what I mean? It's about who they are. It has nothing to do with age!

There's this thing, because I dated Beau [Casper Smart], and he was younger, and he was the first guy I ever dated who was younger than me, but then I got labeled right away. For me, it isn't [about age]. If they're older, they're older. If they're younger, they're younger. It depends on whether or not I'm attracted to their spirit, their soul, their whatever… their energy."

On her tendency to date younger men. February 20, 2017. *ET*

"I still believe in the fairy tale. The more I work on myself, the more I give myself the opportunity to share a really deep and meaningful relationship that can give me my fairy tale and last forever. I believe in marriage; I believe that two people can commit to each other and share a life together. But my main relationship is with myself, and when I'm happy on my own, it will allow for something great to happen.

I have to remind myself not to settle. I know what I have to offer and what I have to give in a relationship. And if I'm going to share my amazing kids and my amazing life and my amazing love, then it has to be amazing in return…. I'm single. I was definitely on lockdown for a while, and now I'm open. But I'm not rushing into anything in any way, shape or form, and I'm not looking."

On being open to love and not allowing herself to become cynical. February 2, 2015. *People magazine*

"We started dating when I was 15 and dated only each other for nine years. We were very careful. I'm not saying we weren't having sex, because we were. We lived in the same neighborhood and he'd see me in, like, a weird hat, wearing something I'd cut together from a picture I'd seen in a magazine and I'd be just going to the track to run. I was creating my own style. Everybody would look at me, like I was a nerd, 'What is she doing? What is she wearing?' Because people didn't do that in my neighborhood. People didn't work out or take care of their bodies. If people see you striving for things, it threatens them. I was into, 'This two-bit town isn't big enough for me.' My boyfriend would say, 'Jennifer has bigger plans.' "

On her first boyfriend, David Cruz. February 1, 1998. *Movieline*

"Both of us being from New York, both being Puerto Rican, was obviously something that connected us from the beginning. The thing with me and Marc from years ago – everybody will always see it – whenever the two of us got in a room together, neither one of us could stop laughing. He comes off as a very serious artist because he is; he's blessed and has a tremendous gift. But because he's so serious, people don't realize because he doesn't give a lot of interviews–he's one of the funniest people you'll ever meet."

On Marc Anthony. April 25, 2006. *People en Español magazine*

"I love getting married. I really want to get married in a church with a big dress."

On having hope that she will find the right matrimonial match in her future. January 5, 2016. *Today*

"I'm open to possibilities. Listen, at the end of the day, love is the best thing. But what I've discovered is that I can't get that from somebody else. It's the love inside me, for myself, that will help me through."

On not giving up on men and love. February 2, 2015. *People magazine*

"I think you both need to run the show sometimes. It has to be a balance, or else it just gets boring. Sometimes I need to be in charge, sometimes he needs to be in charge. It's a partnership. Things just happen, and you're in the middle of it and you just try to navigate your way through it being a good person. Doing the best you can. Trying to learn from the ups and downs. You find you learn a lot more from the downs. When it comes to love and relationships, what I've learned now is that the most important relationship is with myself. And it took me a long time to get to that place. But I finally feel that I understand that. It wasn't anyone else's fault but I couldn't be right in any relationship until I got more in touch with who I was, and what I needed and what I wanted. And getting to that place for me has been the real journey, the real task, where I realize that the main relationship I needed to have and the real love had to be with myself."

On who runs the show in her marriage with Marc Anthony. August 4, 2011. *Vanity Fair*

"We got together and broke up and are now together again. I still think about getting married and having that long life with someone. I love the movie *The Notebook*. A dream of mine is to grow old with someone."

On her on-and-off boyfriend since 2011, Casper Smart. April 13, 2016. *W Magazine*

"It's hard to change our patterns, but when things are not working, you have to look at yourself and ask why. I wanted my relationships to go well, but they were not. There were times when I was just crying to myself: 'I hate this, I hate being alone.' But the goal was not to be alone forever. The goal was to be okay on my own so I can make good choices. When I'm afraid, I just make a silly choice. My [relationship pattern] was, 'Come on in. It doesn't matter how you treat me or what you do. I'm going to accept it because I am so afraid that there will be nobody here.'

But I think in our 20s and 30s we're meant to explore and make a ton of mistakes. And then by our 40s we come more full circle and figure things out. I would have loved for my marriage in my 20s [to chef Ojani Noa in 1997] to last till I died, but I see that maybe that was too early. I had more things to learn, and he had more things to learn. And [same with] the next person I married [actor-choreographer Cris Judd in 2001]. And that's okay. I think we get to a point in our lives where we figure out who we are and then we're great for somebody else. Until then it's going to be a struggle."

On facing her past mistakes when it comes to husbands and boyfriends. February 2, 2015. *People magazine*

"He's adorable. He really is [loving and sweet.] He's a good egg. I don't want to talk about it too much. It's my private thing."

On her boyfriend, Casper Smart. March 15, 2012. *Vogue Magazine*

"I will always respect Marc as a singer and performer. We actually work great together, and he was always *very* supportive. Together we could make magic — and we did. He will always be in our lives. He will always hold a special place in my heart as the father of my children. And out of respect for our family, I will keep private the details of our personal life."

On her feelings for Marc Anthony after the announcement of their divorce. August 4, 2011. *Vanity Fair*

"The best and worst part? I mean, there's no bad part to it, really. It's not about the fact that they're a dancer or not a dancer. I've dated two dancers. One, I had a brief marriage with, Cris Judd, who is an amazing person and whom I love, and then Beau [Smart], who we just broke up, who I love as well. He's a good friend."

On the best and worst thing about dating dancers. June 20, 2014. *E News*

"It matters, especially at the beginning of a relationship. I think to give something a chance, to really get to know somebody, you want to do it out of the public eye. You know the media — they want to rush everything. They want to give their seedy opinions without knowing all the facts. So can I [be private in a relationship]? Yeah. I think so. When I'm ready to do that, I will. But I'm not thinking about that right now."

On whether it matters or is important for her to start a new relationship out of the public eye. October 31, 2011. *Glamour magazine*

"But I also know that I can't make decisions based on the fear. So that when a person does show up, it's not like I have to have them there, or I'm like, 'Yeah this is so nice, let's move in together!' I just go, 'You know, let's get to know each other, let's see if you fit in, are you good enough for my kids?' And if we bump into, you know some bumpy parts, 'Are you gonna work on it with me?'

I'm open to it, I'm open to love, but right now, I think it's better to just be on my own for a minute and learn more about myself."

On being scared to be alone now that she is single again. November 4, 2014. *Today*

"So many things. I knew that he loved and cared about me that much. [It] was like the world stopped when it came to me. And he's Puerto Rican, I'm Puerto Rican, we both grew up in New York — me in the Bronx, and Marc in East Harlem, where my mother grew up."

On what Marc Anthony brought to her life. August 4, 2011. *Vanity Fair*

"A lot of people in my personal life said that I shouldn't have gotten married so fast. This business is tougher on women who are doing better than men because men are raised to be the supporters. We still live with those sensibilities. It's tough for me because the men I'm attracted to, for some reason, haven't gotten it together. Even my husband, I feel, has a lot of potential but he's not at the point where... I mean, even though he has lots of contacts, even though he's doing his own thing, opening a club and restaurant here, whatever business he gets in, he's not gonna make as much money as me. That's something he has to deal with and to live with, which is tough for someone like him.

And, see, I'm not a good example because I'm not normal. I sure wasn't normal at 23, when I was on television and making more than my mom and dad. It's hard for me to find normal contemporaries and it's hard for men to deal with. The man I've married is Latin and they, more than any other type of man, are very macho. I always joke with him, because he's like, 'You can see through that dress!' or 'Is there going to be a love scene in that next movie? You're my wife. I don't want anybody to think of you in that way.' It's just a sweet thing. But I go, 'Look, the love scenes, the see-through dresses--all that stuff is good. As long as people like you, they're going to keep coming to see your movies. Do you want that house in Miami--yes or no?' I mean, this is what it's going to be, it's part of the business."

On her first marriage to Ojani Noa. February 1, 1998. *Movieline*

"I feel like, when we're kids, you're sold into this fairy tale of what love is. That Prince Charming's gonna come along and save you and you're gonna live happily ever after. They're gonna rescue me from the Bronx, and we're gonna go off and live in a castle somewhere and it's gonna be awesome. He's gonna love me forever, and I'm gonna love him forever, and it's gonna be real easy. And it's so different than that."

On the unraveling of her marriage to Marc Anthony. November 4, 2014. *Today*

"I think it's one of the biggest compliments you can give; like you want to feel safe. I'm good here. Unsafe would be bad for me. And over the course of our marriage, there [were] times when I felt the most happiness I ever felt in my life. I always dreamed of having a family, and still being vibrant in my career, and having a partner who did his own things, and doing things together. Making each other bigger. It fulfilled some of my dreams."

On her claim that she felt 'safe' with Marc Anthony and whether feeling safe is a good or bad thing in a relationship. August 4, 2011. *Vanity Fair*

"I do. I'm very old-fashioned and traditional. Maybe I was born at the wrong time."

On whether she believes in old-fashioned romance. January 22, 2001. *The Times-Colonist*

"We try, we try. [But] it's getting increasingly harder. When we were [first] married, most of the time, and even before the babies were born, we were able to go everywhere together. I wasn't working as much. So we kind of had that. I went on tour with him a few times in the first few years of our marriage, and we did a film [*El Cantante*] together. But it's hard, and we're figuring it out. It's tough. And … everything is ramping up in a way. Like I said, we had the first three years of our marriage just for us. I wasn't working, it was really mainly about him. Then we got pregnant. Then it became about the kids. And then I started working again."

On how she and Marc Anthony balance their busy careers, their marriage, and their family. August 4, 2011. *Vanity Fair*

"Without going into detail . . . it's just really, really sad. And look, we are still going through it, and it's emotional sometimes and difficult. We're still friends—and we're parents. But it's going to take time. It's tough. But for the most part, I feel very proud of the way we're handling it. I really do. We are doing the best we can for the kids. What you saw today, on *Ellen,* it's very dignified and trying to be above all the emotions and pain that come along with a divorce and a family breaking apart. This is grown-up stuff. It's real, serious, grown-up stuff."

On her split from Marc Anthony. March 15, 2012. *Vogue Magazine*

"I wasn't in touch with who I was, what I wanted, what I deserved, what I needed. It was more about the other person for me, and that's where I made my mistakes. It wasn't even their fault; it was me. I needed to get to where I could say I know what I want, I know what I need, I can't let you do this, I can't let this happen, I can't let that happen. Even when I felt bad about myself, I always tried to keep in my mind—I'm worth more than this, I'm better than this, I'm doing something that's not right for myself. You deserve better, all the things you have to tell yourself to get through a tough time."

On the pattern in her past of 'choosing men badly.' August 4, 2011. *Vanity Fair*

"It was awful. But I had to make a commitment to myself to be alone: no flirting. No possibility of anything. No boys in any way, shape or form. I said, 'I'm shutting it down.' I'd never been alone. I grew up sleeping in a bed with my two sisters. When I became famous, I was surrounded by people and always had a boyfriend or a husband or some relationship, one after the other. At night I said to myself, 'You're not working, the kids are asleep, what do you like to do, Jen?' I didn't know. It was always, 'What does he want to do? What do the kids want to do?' It was very eye- opening to me to spend time completely by myself. I was terrified of being alone: The idea that we are alone in this world, we were born alone, we die alone—it sent panic through my body. I said, 'I have to face this fear,' and I did."

On being truly alone for the first time after her divorce with Marc Anthony and her relationship with Casper Smart ended. February 2, 2015. *People magazine*

"I think that I've finally learned the biggest lesson of all. You've got to love yourself first. You've got to be okay on your own before you can be okay with somebody else. You've got to value yourself and know that you're worth *everything*. And until you value yourself enough and love yourself enough to know that, you can't really have a healthy relationship."

On what she has learned from past relationships that have prepared her for new relationships. October 31, 2011. *Glamour magazine*

"I love that song and felt it was a good transition into the next part of the show. I fell in love with this thing choreographer Parris Goebel did with Etta James' music, and I said, 'I want to do something like that to my song.' So she choreographed it. And Casper was like, 'I want to do it too.' We did it together, and it just seemed very natural."

On the erotic dance she did with her boyfriend Casper Smart while on stage as she sang *Baby I Love U!*. December 6, 2013. *Elle Canada*

"Marc and I are good how we are right now. There's a reason we're not together, but we're great friends. And we're parents together. We're even working on a Spanish album together.

That has been even better for us. We met working, and that's where we're really magical. When we're on stage together, and so we leave it there. That's it."

On whether she and Marc Anthony would ever get back together again. March 4, 2017. *People magazine*

SHOW BUSINESS

"I think I'm a really great performer. I think I'm a really great actress. I feel confident in those things — that's a better way to say it. I'm not as gifted a vocalist as some of the girls that are out there, but I know I communicate. When I think of great vocalists, I think of Marc, of Luther Vandross, of Whitney Houston. But Marc has helped me a lot with this; he always said I had a beautiful voice and that it was better than I thought it was."

On what she considers her greatest talent. August 4, 2011. *Vanity Fair*

"You know, I have had such a good time doing comedies. I really want to kind of spread my wings in that area a little bit. So I'm looking at a bunch of comedies right now. I love the drama and I know, you know, some of my fans really like when I do that. But I - I really feel like it's a great time to kind of, you know, really explore comedy a little bit more. I'm really enjoying that. So that's what I'm looking at right now. So I think that's what you'll probably see me in next."

On the future movie roles she wants to try. June 16, 2010. *CNN*

"This tour was therapy. It was a case of, pick yourself up and dance again. That's why this documentary was born, it was an account of survival."

On her HBO documentary *Dance Again*. October 21, 2015. *Huffington Post UK*

"When I first started in music, Puffy and I were together and he mentored me. He let me know what the music business was like, and that was something that I took with me. I didn't think about it at the time, but then I realized later I'm quoting him!"

On what advice she got when she first started in show business. October 31, 2011. *Glamour magazine*

"It's set in the world of cops, but it's really about human nature – how we're always riding a line of what's right and what's wrong, that slippery slope."

On the TV show she stars in, *Shades of Blue*. January 22, 2016. *The Independent*

"Awful."

On Ben Affleck's relatively new enormous tattoo. April 13, 2016. *W Magazine*

"I started as a dancer, so I have an eye for it. I've done it my whole life. Sometimes other people – the music department, or my management – might like a person, but I'm, like, 'Oh, they're a little bit weak in this part, there's not enough technique.' "

On choosing back-up dancers for her Vegas show. January 22, 2016. *The Independent*

"I think I paved the way for them. Just another innovation that I've given to the world!"

On whether the Kardashians stole her jam with their great asses. April 13, 2016. *W Magazine*

"I want [the show] to be a high-energy, Bronx kind of block-party. The most exciting shows make you dance, and scream and jump up and down. I want people to really let loose. It's always been my approach to performing, to work, to everything I do in life: I give it all I have. That's why it's the name of my show."

On her Vegas show opening late January 2016; her show is called *All I Have*. January 22, 2016. *The Independent*

"It was an amazing time in my life, let alone my career, you know just to be able to be involved with that project and play Selena. It was just a great time and it was one of my first leading roles. I'll never forget it."

On her experience making the movie *Selena*. May 7, 2014. 99.7 Now! New Hit Music

"I've been in the grind and the game for a long time. At a certain point, people respect you when they see you fall down and get back up. The more you're in this life, the more they celebrate your triumphs. When it comes to work, I never get tired."

On being in the business for a considerable length of time. April 13, 2016. *W Magazine*

"Because I'm the best. I feel I can do anything - any kind of role. I'm fearless. I work really hard. I'll just get better as I go along because I'm open to getting better. If you have the goods, there's nothing to be afraid of. If somebody doesn't have the goods, they're insecure. I don't have that problem. I'm not the best actress that ever lived, but I know I'm pretty good."

On how she pulled off her recent string of movie hits. February 1, 1998. *Movieline*

"It's really about when you meet somebody and you finally feel like, ok, this is it, this is the one. This is the one. This is the real thing, and wishing you had met them years before."

On the meaning behind her song *First Love*. May 7, 2014. 99.7 Now! New Hit Music

"I was always fascinated by how I could see [a man] being late or being belligerent to a crew and it being totally acceptable; meanwhile, I'd show up 15 minutes late and be berated. Like, we're not allowed to have certain opinions or even be passionate about something, or they'll be like, 'God, she's really difficult.' It's like, 'Am I? Am I difficult because I care?'
"

On being labeled a diva. May 19, 2016. *Popsugar*

"All your creative ideas get pared back, little by little, because it gets very expensive to put everything on a boat to China or Australia. In Vegas, though, you're in one place, so I get to dream – the ideas I have [for sets] can come to life in a way they never have before. That's why some of the best shows are in Vegas."

On how her residency in Vegas allows her more creative freedom than touring from venue to venue. January 22, 2016. *The Independent*

"Are those the only choices? Not in a bad way! Just, you know—there's so many booties!

You know who I'm going to say has a great booty that I've seen in person? What's her name? Jessica Biel! She has an amazing body. I remember seeing her and going, 'God, she has a really nice, toned body. I need to go back to the gym!' "

On whether Beyonce or Kim Kardashian comes closer to rivaling her booty. June 20, 2014. *E News*

"I'm very comfortable with being *productive*. I like doing things, and I like creating things. As far as being powerful, I guess I'm comfortable with it. It's not really how I think of myself."

On being powerful. October 31, 2011. *Glamour magazine*

"In videos and things that I do, I'm very sexy and wear little clothes, but the truth is, when it comes to acting, I did it earlier in my career and now I just don't feel sometimes that you have to do it. I've changed in that sense."

On nudity in her work. May 18, 2016. *The Hollywood Reporter*

"I'm not as gifted a vocalist as some of the girls out there, but I know I communicate. It's a much more intimate experience, and it's about real performers. Not everybody can really do that."

On performing in her Vegas show. January 22, 2016. *The Independent*

"When you love something you never get tired of it. You just want to keep growing and evolving and doing it and staying here."

On still loving her career, even after all these years. 2014. 97.1 AMP Radio

"Do I think she's a great performer? Yeah. Do I think she's a great actress? No. Acting is what I do, so I'm harder on people when they say, 'Oh, I can do that - I can act.' I'm like, 'Hey, don't spit on my craft.' "

On fellow actress and performer Madonna. February 1, 1998. *Movieline*

"The fun part of the entertainment business for me is the fantasy. The fairy tale and the magic. I haven't lost touch with the little girl in me. I love fancy, frilly, and sparkly things. It's part of being a girl."

On having rows of gowns, shoes, and other tangible symbols of her success. August 4, 2011. *Vanity Fair*

"Just the title, *First Love*, you think of so many different visuals that can go with that. The song gives you a feeling more than anything, because it's gonna mean so many different things for so many different people. It's not about your first love; it's just, 'I wish you were the person I had met early and then I wouldn't have had to go through all these things.' I just think that was such a beautiful sentiment."

On her song *First Love*. June 19, 2014. *Fuse*

"I really love them. You look to your left and your right and you see a smile and feel the warmth. It's a good feeling."

On her relationship between the other judges and herself on *American Idol*. March 15, 2012. *Vogue Magazine*

"I love working with the singers. I love just finding them. This week, Scotty McCreery's album is number one! And we discovered him.

It's such a great exchange, because in helping the contestants, you grow yourself in a weird way. You're watching them, going, 'You know what? I do that sometimes.' "

On what she loves most about doing *American Idol*. October 31, 2011. *Glamour magazine*

"I learned a lot from that time in my life where I did overstretch myself. I can handle it better because I go, 'No, I'm not going to work on that day,' or 'No, I am going to take those three days off,' or, 'No, you cannot schedule that there,' And you realise the sky is not going to fall, even though everybody makes you feel like it's going to."

On learning that she needs to take a break sometimes instead of working nonstop. November 11, 2015. *Marie Claire*

"That was the big thing from the word go. To make her a real person. If she's not, then people can't identify with her. Being an impersonation would have been a huge mistake. And bad acting. So, I just approached her like I do all my characters: research. Everything I could find on her: interviews, behind-the-scenes stuff, anything. Any little insight into her personality: how she acted differently in performance than she did in interviews, how her English interviews differed from her Spanish interviews... All sorts of shades that were important for me to get there."

On making Selena a real person instead of an impression when she filmed *Selena*. 2008. *Film Scouts*

"I love what I do, and I feel so fortunate to do it for so long and to keep being inspired and to keep trying to push the envelope and to keep trying to be better — not just as performer and an actress and a singer, but also as a person."

On not feeling like being busy is a burden. March 2, 2017. *Today*

"I'm going to perform all my chart hits, not a bunch of album cuts no one knows."

On what she is going to perform during her Vegas shows. January 22, 2016. *The Independent*

"People are paying, and it has to be the best it can possibly be. You want people to have the best night of their life. That's what inspired me to do this, to give people a place to escape, to forget everything else, to be inspired themselves. That's your role, your responsibility as a performer.

I'm driven in that way. That's what makes an artist. People in this business understand that, and everyone in the team pushes and pushes. They're all artists. They want to be driven, everyone's seeking perfection."

On wanting to make every show on her tour the best it can possibly be. October 21, 2015. *Huffington Post UK*

"I think it's a little bit much. I don't think I'm any racier than any other female pop artist. Okay, I'll wear a sexy outfit, but I think it's more because my body shape's a little different to other body shapes, so that's not very fair."

On the list of complaints to Ofcom regarding an outfit she wore, a leather thong swimsuit and feather bolero. June 19, 2013. *The Telegraph*

"I've run into that trouble in Vegas before. It's super-dry so you have to take care of yourself and have tons of humidifiers. I also use masks to replenish [skin] moisture. They look like bandages."

On working in Vegas, where the constant air-conditioning and the dry desert air can be brutal for vocal cords. January 22, 2016. *The Independent*

"I love Drake. He's so brilliant. Talented. Amazing. We made a song together and um... We hung out. We have a great time. And he's amazing. I have so much love for him."

On Drake. February 21, 2017. *Elle*

"When I was presented the opportunity to work with Endless, based upon Jesper Nielsen's previous history and knowing the company's reputation for delivering quality product, their management skills and their relationship with retailers, I felt the combination would be a very successful brand extension. As an entertainer and as a woman, Endless Jewelry's concept gives me an opportunity to express myself. In turn, it gives other women an opportunity to express themselves through the charms, which they can mix and match in countless ways. This allows for an endless number of custom designs that are tailored to the individual."

On being the brand ambassador and co-designer of Endless Jewelry. January 6, 2016. *The Star*

"He has a lot of strength and we got along great, actually. He could tell right away I wasn't intimidated to be there with him and Oliver [Stone]. I remember asking him, 'Why do we always see pictures of you looking like you're ready to hit somebody?' and he goes, 'Because in those pictures, I'm never with my friends.' "

On fellow actor Sean Penn. February 1, 1998. *Movieline*

"I've been in the music business for years. I know what it is to audition, to perform, to write a song and record and tour. I have something to say, and you never get to talk about stuff like that."

On knowing she would be able to bring something fresh to *American Idol* if she took on the role of a judge. March 15, 2012. *Vogue Magazine*

"It's a bad feeling. It's a bad feeling. Even to act, it's a bad feeling. ... That's why I said, emotionally, this was the hardest movie I've done, and the most challenging for me because I've never been in a relationship where there was any physical contact like that, so it was hard, you know what I mean, to really go there."

On the scenes in *Enough* where her character was being physically abused; they were challenging for her to film. April 25, 2002. *Puerto Rico Herald*

"I was never a big fan of hers. In Hollywood she's revered, she gets nominated for Oscars, but I've never heard anyone in the public or among my friends say, 'Oh, I love her.' She's cute and talented, though, and I'd like her just for looking like my older sister, Leslie."

On fellow actress Winona Ryder. February 1, 1998. *Movieline*

"I had really wanted to work with Max for many, many years, and it just never happened. For [*A.K.A.*], I was like, 'I want to work with you.' I met with him in the summertime, and he was like, 'I'm just going off to do Adele's album!' or somebody he works with all the time. I was like, 'When are you back?' ... I was like, 'I'll wait for you.' "

On her eagerness to work with famed songwriter and producer Max Martin. June 19, 2014. *Fuse*

"It's bull. Sure, you can dress nicely after a couple of months and people will say, 'Oh, look how amazing they look in a picture taken from a good angle.' But the truth is it takes your body time to go back, and I think these days women are too hard on themselves with that.

Nobody bounces back straightaway. You don't know what kind of Spanx these women are wearing under their clothes, and what other tricks are going on."

On the current trend with celebrities to get back to their pre-pregnancy body very quickly after giving birth. June 19, 2013. *The Telegraph*

"I did kind of like, say, 'You're a movie star! You should wear a suit! You should do this with your hair!' For sure. I mean, I do that. By the way, guys do that to girls, too: 'I like that dress better than the other dress.' [Affleck] was into it. He didn't do anything he didn't want to do...He had some good fashion moments when he was with me!"

On whether she dressed Ben Affleck when the two of them were dating. June 20, 2014. *E News*

"When I first started, the only roles I would get offered was as a maid. People would look at my name and discount me from bigger roles. Other Latino actresses such as Ava Gardner (born Margarita Cansino) and Raquel Welch (Requel Tejada) changed their names but I was determined not to do that. I am very proud of who I am.

In Hollywood most of the big female stars are very thin, flat-chested blondes. People always say I am a big girl but it's just by comparison I look voluptuous. But I love that people think I am sexy. I am happy to use my body but I never abuse it. People go on about me being sexy and some get the wrong idea. I refuse to go naked in a movie. I have had it written into contracts that I won't do nude scenes. I think leaving something to the imagination is far more sensual."

On her acting roles when she first started acting. June 18, 1999. *The Mirror*

"Oliver Stone's film has Sean Penn, Nick Nolte and myself. It's a film noir. Weird. Good. It's set in present day, but it's small town, so it's a little bit out of time. I play an Apache Indian."

On the Oliver Stone movie she made, *U-Turn*. 2008. *Film Scouts*

"This was one of the first things with my production company that I felt like, 'This is something I really want to make. This is something I really want to make.' The script was brought to me, I guess, about four or five years ago now, through Puchi, who had done interviews with the very first writer on the screenplay, David [Darmstaedter], and David Maldonado brought it to my manager at the time, saying 'Read it, it's the Hector Lavoe story, and Puchi wants Jennifer to play her.' I read it, and I'll be honest, much like when I did Selena, I knew of the music, and I knew a little bit of the story, but I didn't know the whole story. When I read it, and started learning more about it, I just became obsessed and impassioned with the whole idea of the project and their lives. And once I really got to know the music, I was like, 'Wow! This is important.' And then, it being a Puerto Rican story, and my production company being Nuyorican Productions, what better movie to be the first movie for Nuyorican Productions than this?"

On starring in and producing *El Cantante*, a bio-pic about the rise and fall of Hector Lavoe, a celebrated salsa singer from the seventies (Marc Anthony plays the title role while Lopez plays Puchi, his long-suffering wife.) No date. Aalbc.com

"I'm up to seven or eight fragrances now."

On her hugely profitable fragrance lines. October 6, 2008. *The Daily Beast*

"I've played about ten cops in my career."

On the research she did to play a police officer in *Shades of Blue*. June 16, 2016. *Deadline*

"Tell me what she's been in? I swear to God, I don't remember anything she was in. Some people get hot by association. I heard more about her and Brad Pitt than I ever heard about her work."

On fellow actress Gwyneth Paltrow. February 1, 1998. *Movieline*

"Well, you know to me, it is not that big a deal because I was always very athletic. So to me the athletic stuff is fun. I'm like, 'Let me jump over the fence, please.' "

On performing her own stunts in her movie *Angel Eyes*. May 17, 2017. *ABC News*

"We spent three years of our lives together, you know almost every single day. As much as he roots for me and as proud as he is of me and of the time we had together, I am just as proud to see what he's done.

Seeing him involved in Revolt and all the things that he's done as a business man and still being so true to his music and his art trying to uplift his community in his own way, and it's the same thing that I try to do and I feel like I learned a lot from him coming up, watching him."

On Sean 'Diddy' Combs, who Lopez dated in the 1990s. October 2, 2014. *Daily Mail*

"I've always been a hard worker. I've worked hard for many, many years now and to be at a point in my career where I've been in it for 20-something years and be getting the opportunities and me having a moment like this where I get to as an artist do all the things that I love to do still ... All of it feels like such a blessing."

On her career currently. March 31, 2016. *People magazine*

"I started developing the movie in 2002. Héctor's wife, Puchi, was working on the script in conjunction with writer David Maldonado and they brought it to me. Puchi wanted me to play her and I read it. I called Marc [Anthony] four years ago; we weren't even seeing each other then at that time or even talking. I called his manager and said 'Look, there's this part I know Marc is born to play and I'll be playing his wife,' and four years later it all just happened. When we did the movie we were married, which is really crazy."

On her movie *El Cantante*. April 25, 2006. *People en Español magazine*

"Women in general, but also artists — they're always put in a box, you know what I mean? […] when I started acting [people would say] 'You can't record an album.' And I was like, 'No, no, no really, I want to record an album. I really, I can do it. I can do it. I promise.' And then it was like, okay so then I got the chance to do that. And then it was like, okay I'll do my live shows. Okay, I want to do branding. I want to create a perfume. You know I worked in a perfume store when I was sixteen and I have a lot of ideas!"

On having to work at not being compartmentalized in the entertainment industry. March 8, 2017. *Vibe*

"I don't have a feud against her at all. I know from back in the day, I've read things that she's said about me that were not the greatest, but we have never met. Like, we don't know each other. I think it's kind of from word of mouth of things that have happened in the past that I'm not really aware of. But I don't know.

I would love to meet her and I would love to be friends with her. I think she's incredibly talented and I've always been a fan of hers. *My All* is one of my favorite songs of all time. I just love her. It saddens me to hear anything that's negative because I'm a fan of hers."

On the alleged feud between herself and Mariah Carey. June 20, 2014. *E News*

"I see myself as the creative chief officer of my life. Anything I get involved with, whether it's business, music, movies or producing, it all comes from what's important to me. That's what makes a brand that has DNA to it. All great businesses have great partners, great collaborators who really know the businesses you are getting into. But you have to have chemistry with them."

On the J-Lo brand. July 14, 2012. *Stylist magazine*

"We haven't been onstage together for about five years. It was good. You know, he came to my show in Vegas, to see it; we've been talking about doing something.

He said, 'I'm doing Radio City, will you do one of the nights with me?' I was like, 'Yeah, I'll be in New York, I can do it,' so it just worked out really well.

We're talking about doing some stuff together... We don't have anything to announce at this moment, but soon."

On Lopez and ex-husband Marc Anthony performing together during Anthony's concert at the Radio City Music Hall in New York City. September 2, 2016. *The Brampton Guardian*

"I wanted an extravaganza, something really where people go OMG, you have to see this.

I'll give it all I have. Everything I've ever done has led to this. I've spent my entire life waiting for this moment to create my own show. It's going to be the best J.Lo show you've ever seen and heard. It will be with all my hits. We have a lot of different things to try to do on that stage.

There's so much there in Las Vegas. Think of it as one super party you've wanted to go to your entire life. I'm just going to heighten the experience so that everybody has a good time. There's a lot of new technology that will fit the personality and concept of the show. I'm going to keep asking what new thing can we bring to the stage.

I can't tell you how excited I am about this Las Vegas residency. The only thing that worries me is that I love all the great restaurants and shopping on the Strip. So I'm going to have to be very careful not to eat too much or to shop too much. That's the only problem I think I'll have!"

On her Vegas stage show. January 20, 2016. *Las Vegas Sun*

"He's such a powerful vocalist, and he always believed in me as a vocalist and he knew it was a confidence thing for me. While we were married, he really helped me with that. And once I toured for the first time, I realized I was a much stronger vocalist than I gave myself credit for. [After the tour] I just couldn't wait to get into the studio. There was nothing to be afraid of. I had to really push myself."

On Marc Anthony helping her gain confidence in her vocal ability. June 12, 2014. *Los Angeles Times*

"You have to develop a way of dealing with it, and my way of dealing with it is to not even know what's going on. So I don't know half the things they (the media) say or half the things they write or the rumours that are out there. I don't care. I don't care to know. I don't ask anybody what's going on."

On how she deals with negative publicity. January 22, 2001. *The Times-Colonist*

"I wanted it to be beautiful and sexy, not sexy and raunchy. Sometimes when you're younger, you go for raunch, or shock value, but I don't need to do that. I did sexy things but I was always more the good girl who was falling in love as opposed to the naughty girl who was running around."

On her infamous video for *Booty* with Iggy Azalea (which features Lopez and Iggy writhing around in oil) that some people felt was too raunchy. November 11, 2015. *Marie Claire*

"Do I want to sit there again or do I want to keep going with what I'm doing? And the truth is, I'm not a TV personality. I'm a singer. I'm a dancer. I'm an actress. I'm an entertainer. I need to entertain. When I'm watching them up there, I'm thinking about what I'm going to be doing next, do you know what I mean?"

On whether she wants to do another season of *American Idol*. 2014. 97.1 AMP Radio

"Whenever I am recording songs, I think to myself, are girls going to wanna scream this at the top of their lungs? You know what I mean? Are they gonna want to sing this in their car? That's always one of my criteria."

On what is important to her when writing songs. May 7, 2014. 99.7 Now! New Hit Music

"I like to make jokes. I like to make people laugh - absolutely. So I wanted a chance to show I was goofy. I also wanted a chance to do a romantic comedy. I wanted to see how it would be. I was nervous and scared, because you don't know whether you will be funny on screen.

I'm just where Mary (Lopez's character in *The Wedding Planner*) was in her life - being so focused on her career ... and having no other life besides. I mean, her whole life was her work - and I could relate to that."

On her movie *The Wedding Planner*. January 22, 2001. *The Times-Colonist*

"When you act, you play a part. But when you sing, it is just you. I feel very liberated when I sing and I just love it."

On wanting to expand her career from acting into a singing career as well. June 18, 1999. *The Mirror*

"That's always been something I've wanted to do, to broaden the scope."

On playing a psychologist in the movie *The Cell*. August 5, 2000. *The Spectator*

"I think that's kind of over. Women have taken over the music industry – when you think of all the female artists who are out. Even going back 20 years, back to Cher, Gloria Estefan and that whole time with Mariah Carey and Celine Dion and then the next wave which was me and Britney and Beyoncé to what's continued to now with Rihanna and Lady Gaga. With all these people there have been a few guys but we have really had it on lock for a little bit."

On whether sexism is as prevalent in the music industry as it used to be. July 14, 2012. *Stylist magazine*

"There are certain people that are marked for death already. I have my little list of journalists that have treated me unfairly. Like, I was totally happy, totally confident with my work in *Selena*, but out of the 700 reviews - and I read every single one - I can quote the one who said, *The one thing you don't do when you walk out of this movie is say, 'Who's that girl?'* I was like, 'You lying bitch!' When another person from that same magazine came up to me, the first thing I said to her was, 'You tell that other bitch that writes for your magazine that I'm never talking with her again.' I definitely have my list of people that are going to get their justice."

On treatment of her by the press. February 1, 1998. *Movieline*

"It's been like that since *Selena*. I never thought about fame until then. After that film, I would have panic attacks. I remember walking down the street, and someone yelled, 'Jennifer!' and I didn't know who it was. I ran home. From that point forward, I realized I couldn't be alone in public. I don't think I've been alone on the street in over 20 years."

On her fame and being mobbed whenever she goes out in public. April 13, 2016. *W Magazine*

"I've done some movies that I'm very proud of — and I have been in some movies that were not so great. But I feel I am at a perfect time in my life to wait for the right role, one I can really sink my teeth into. But I have to be patient and know that that's coming, instead of doing things just to do them."

On wanting to make the right movie role choices. March 15, 2012. *Vogue Magazine*

"I was really drawn to the love story in it. Two people from kind of tragic backgrounds in a way who never were able to move on from their past, and through the love that they have for each other, they are able to heal each other and move on, you know, and actually have a life after so many years and leave the past behind them."

On her movie *Angel Eyes*. May 17, 2017. *ABC News*

"He's a wild man. He doesn't hide anything when it comes to sex in his life. He loves women, he has a lot of sex. He loves talking about how he sleeps with women. Like he'll come onto the set going, 'Aggghh, I was up fucking until four in the morning until I passed out.' Oliver is a great guy, highly sexual, and he was so good to me making the movie. Oh, and something else - I'm attracted to scent and he smells really great, like spicy lavender. You know what those expensive purple candies smell like in your mouth? The ones nobody has here but you can get in New York and Europe? That's what he smells like."

On Oliver Stone, a movie director that she worked with on *U Turn*. February 1, 1998. *Movieline*

"I have mixed feelings to it ending – it's a big celebration, but it's melancholy at the same time. But something else will come up."

On how she feels about her five year stint on *American Idol* coming to an end. January 22, 2016. *The Independent*

"Broadway musicals and films fueled my childhood and *Bye Bye Birdie* was one of my favourites. I'm proud to be a part of the NBC family with *Shades of Blue* and I thought it would be a blast to take on one of their big live musicals."

On her stint playing the role of Rose 'Rosie' Alvarez in the live production of *Bye Bye Birdie* in 2017 as well as taking on the role of executive producer of the musical. October 28, 2016. *The Brampton Guardian*

"It's a wig. It was such a good wig."

On her horrible haircut in the second half of the movie *Enough*. May 22, 2002. *National Post*

"When you've been in the business as long as I've been, you get to the point where you think 'OK, I'm here to stay.' As a new artist you always think it could all be over tomorrow. But if you have built a career you get to a point where you think I am going to have some great successes and I am going to have some things that don't work out but it's okay. I'll be alright, no matter what happens. I have my kids, I have my family, I am loved and I have been very successful and I am very fortunate."

On how important critical and commercial success are to her. July 14, 2012. *Stylist magazine*

"It's like all that hard work and now something permanent is going to be there. I made my mark."

On getting a star on the Hollywood Walk of Fame. August 4, 2011. *Vanity Fair*

"It was the first venture I was involved with that turned into a billion dollar business. (Lopez first launched the perfume Glow by J-Lo in 2002.) Even though it didn't make *me* a billionaire, I was proud of that. It won lots of awards so it was groundbreaking."

On which of her fragrances she is most proud of. July 14, 2012. *Stylist magazine*

"A legend in his own time and in his own mind - like the rest of us are peons."

On fellow actor Jack Nicholson. February 1, 1998. *Movieline*

"We don't. We're not really allowed to because we're judges to show any favoritism or anything, so we don't interact with them. We can talk with them on the show. We can say whatever we want to them when we're judging them but for the most part, we're not really allowed to interact."

On how involved the judges on *American Idol* get with the contestants. May 7, 2014. 99.7 Now! New Hit Music

"It goes through the major relationships in my life. I'll be honest: when they (songwriting team APLUS and Bieber/Rihanna producer D'Mile) first wrote the song for me, it was very generic. I loved the idea, though, so I said, 'Why don't we make it more 'me'?' I sat there and wrote the verses with them, and we went through every major relationship I've ever had, asking the question, 'Is there one love?' "

On her song *One Love*. April 20, 2011. *Rolling Stone magazine*

"That would have to be a tie between Woody and Wesley (her *Money Train* co-stars). Woody was more playful, but if I'd have gone for it, he totally would have. I'd say, 'Hey, Woody, how are you doing?' He'd, like, stick out his tongue and flick it at me very nasty.

Harrelson was really funny about it. But Wesley - even though I had a boyfriend at the time - went full court press. He was flirting with me - you always flirt with your co-stars, it's harmless - then he just started getting a little more serious. He would invite us all out together and then at the end of the night, he'd drop me off last and try to kiss me. I'd be like, 'Wesley, please, I'm not interested in you like that.' He got really upset about it. His ego was totally bruised. He wouldn't talk to me for two months. I was like, 'What an asshole.' Actors are used to getting their way and to treating women like objects. They're so used to hearing the word 'Yes.' Now, I suppose Wesley will call me going, 'You bitch! How dare you? I didn't like you.' "

On who in show business has made the clumsiest sexual passes at her. February 1, 1998. *Movieline*

"I have a certain sensibility about the way I dress and design, and I just kind of handed that to him (designer Giuseppe Zanotti). People really associate me with sparkle and a little bit of street edge and things like that. I wanted to make sure the collection had that, but then some [styles] feel very glam and high-end fashion."

On her footwear collection, Giuseppe for Jennifer Lopez. November 17, 2016. *The Brampton Guardian*

"For me, love is the never-ending question. It is confusing. It is the answer, but it is also inundated with contradictions and complications. It's about years of experience in different relationships, and kind of the culmination of that, and how even to this day, I'm still learning."

On why her album titled *Love?* has a question mark. August 2, 2010. *Glamour magazine*

"I think because I do a lot of different things, I don't get credit for being great at one thing like some people are. Somebody once told me, 'One of the best things is when people underestimate you, because then you can always surprise them.' "

On being a mixed-medium artist. June 12, 2014. *Los Angeles Times*

"It's funny: those guys and Ryan (Seacrest) – I really see us as a foursome – we just hit it off right away. There was a lot of mutual respect, and that respect grew into love; we've kind of become like brothers and sisters. They're very protective of me, as I am of them. Our first press conference, this reporter tried to get out of line, and they were like 'Hey! Hey! *Hey!*' I was like, 'I love this!' "

On her initial rapport with fellow judges Steven Tyler and Randy Jackson on *American Idol*. April 20, 2011. *Rolling Stone magazine*

"I honestly thought people knew that I was a good person and a hard worker even though there was all this tabloid, diva stuff about me. I thought they already knew me from being in the public eye for so long. But I guess they really didn't. Reality television really shows you for who you are. And I loved it in the beginning, it was the best thing ever. So much fun, the easiest job. Then by the last few weeks I just got tired. I had never done live TV. I was very attached [to the show]. And by Fridays, I'd be knocked out. It's almost like a fighter after a fight; do you want to go back in and fight again? I'm honestly on the fence about it. I know it's a great thing, but I really have to think — am I going to be happy? Is this going to take me away from a film I want to do? Or a tour? In the end, I [always] just go with my gut."

On people seeing a side of her that they hadn't seen before she was on *American Idol*. August 4, 2011. *Vanity Fair*

"*Shades of Blue* is a cop show, but it's really a show about human nature. It's about people; it's about what they would do when put to the test on certain things, how you can be a good person and really do fucked up things. And we do all the time."

On her TV show *Shades of Blue*. June 16, 2016. *Deadline*

"We're in two different realms. She's a sexy bombshell and those are the kinds of roles she does. I do all kinds of different things. It makes me laugh when she says she got offered *Selena*, which was an outright lie. If that's what she does to get herself publicity, then that's her thing. Columbia offered me the choice of *Fools Rush In* or *Anaconda*, but I chose the fun B-movie because the *Fools* script wasn't strong enough."

On fellow actress Salma Hayek. February 1, 1998. *Movieline*

"She was so cute. We bonded so much. We were good friends. I used to call her 'Angel Princess,' and when I would forget, she'd say, 'How come you didn't call me Angel Princess today?' "

On the four-year-old girl who played her daughter in *Enough*. May 22, 2002. *National Post*

"*The Fosters* is about a kind of unconventional foster family – two women who are in a relationship, one used to be married and has a son so they raise a son together and then they adopt twins and then they start building this family. It's very indicative of our times. Family, for me, is about love and we go about making our own families as we go in life. We have our natural born families, but it's the family you make that raises you and shapes you. Because 'different' things can be looked at in a prejudiced sort of way, whether it's being adopted or being gay, when people watch something it helps them get past their preconceptions and they start looking at people as people – all of us have a worth, a value, a heart and a soul."

On the TV show *The Fosters* that Lopez's production company (Nuyorican Productions) made. July 14, 2012. *Stylist magazine*

"When we announced the role, I actually had anxiety for a couple of nights... It's intense. It's scary to go into those places sometimes. I know what it is to do that as an actor, what it takes."

On playing notorious drug lord Griselda Blanco in an HBO movie. September 2, 2016. *The Brampton Guardian*

"Leslie is kind of at the lowest point of her life. She was married for years; she was kind of a golden girl in her town. But years later she lives with her mother, and it's not so shiny and new anymore. She sees no way out. Finally, this thing comes along and she's so desperate that she'll do anything to make something happen. And you realize that she has not given up. She will do what she has to do to survive, to have her spirit survive. That's how I played her."

On her character, Leslie, in the movie *Parker*, which came out in 2012. March 15, 2012. *Vogue Magazine*

"I've already started mapping that out. You've got to do your share of commercial movies - romantic comedies, action movies - the $100-million movies, because if you don't you're not going to have the power and Hollywood is not going to respect you. I would also do any small, independent movie that appeals to me dramatically, because it keeps everybody realizing that your acting chops are there. I think some actors are making a big mistake by doing one big commercial movie after another. It just looks like you're for sale. People want to know that you're selective."

On her career strategy. February 1, 1998. *Movieline*

"It's always a natural thing I find with actors, if you have chemistry or not. And I always say you can create some, but innately, there has to be a rapport, an easiness, a respect. I feel like we were willing to open up to each other and be those people to each other."

On the powerful on-screen chemistry she shares with her co-star in *Shades of Blue*, Ray Liotta. June 16, 2016. *Deadline*

"It didn't make me re-think anything, really: I kept doing what I was doing, and *Idol* just got added into the mix. I'm sure all those people watching doesn't hurt! But at the end of the day, it comes down to the music: either they like it, or they don't. I'm just happy they like it."

On whether working on *American Idol* made her rethink her own music career. April 20, 2011. *Rolling Stone magazine*

"I did a couple of dance records and people want me to do a dance album. Or they think I should go back to being 'Jenny From the Block.' I am dance, I am pop, I am R&B, I am hip-hop, I am Latin, I am 'Jenny From the Block.' But I am also 'Jenny From Rodeo Drive.' It was about embracing all those things musically, everything about me emotionally, and putting that into lyrics and sound for this album."

On her album *A.K.A.* June 12, 2014. *Los Angeles Times*

"I realized how much I love performing. It's funny, I think when a wardrobe assistant or a make-up artist has to come up onstage, they do this freeze thing and I realized how natural it is for me to be up there and how not natural it is [for them]."

On what her recent world tour taught her. 2014. 97.1 AMP Radio

"A lucky model who's been given a lot of opportunities I just wish she would have done more with. She's beautiful and has a great presence, though, and in *My Best Friend's Wedding*, I thought, 'When directed, she can be good.' "

On fellow actress Cameron Diaz. February 1, 1998. *Movieline*

"While I was shooting *Shades (of Blue)*, I was doing *American Idol* on the weekends. But we were also planning my Vegas show at that time. Then I went home and rehearsed for five weeks, and then we were live on the show. So it was a challenging year. It was a lot of work for me, but I just tried to stay focused when I was on set.

I just tried to be grateful for the fact that, at this point in my career, I have this much going on. But the truth is the quality of the work, of the writing, of the actors, of Barry [Levinson], of the producers, of the writers room—I felt like, this is my best work, you know? This was how I started my career. This is who I am. I always saw myself as an actress who danced and sang and had those talents as well, and I made my records later in my career. I didn't make my first record until I was almost 30. So the acting was always the first thing. That was where people got to know me."

On how she balances *Shades of Blue* with her other work commitments. June 16, 2016. *Deadline*

"I love how spontaneous he is, and that he has a colorful way about him, which adds color to the panel. He's also a very deep and soulful person – the crazy mixed in with that is a beautiful combination."

On being just as surprised as everyone else by the words the come out of Steven Tyler's mouth on *American Idol*. April 20, 2011. *Rolling Stone magazine*

"People think I'm 'nice,' but they still act surprised when I'm smart. It's a man's world, and, truly, people in a business setting do not value a woman as much as a man. I feel like I'm constantly having to prove myself. If a man does one thing well, people immediately say he's a genius. Women have to do something remarkable over and over and over. And, even then, they get questions about their love life. People underestimate me. They always have, and maybe that's for the best. It's fun to prove them wrong."

On being a woman in show business. April 13, 2016. *W Magazine*

QUOTES ABOUT LOPEZ

"I am such a fan of Jennifer Lopez. I think she's the Sophia Loren of our generation. There was a time in the record industry when this was considered the singing business. But it is no longer just the singing business; we're in the entertainment business, and it's the total package. Jennifer's songs and performances are believable. Also, she is such a sweetheart, such a joy to work with. *American Idol* was an amazing platform for her."

Antonio "L.A." Reid (now the head of Epic Records), who signed Lopez in March 2010 when he was the chairman of Island Def Jam. August 4, 2011. *Vanity Fair*

"The thing that I always sort of wished is that she would give herself time to just naturally meet someone instead of having nearly obsessive guys pursue her. The ease with which that obsession becomes a relationship I think sometimes works against her ability to have a real meaningful relationship. And she never half does anything. When she commits to anything in her work, her life, or her relationships, she is in it. I'm not telling you anything I haven't told her. And I think to her detriment, the will of Jennifer is so strong that she believes that it can actually change who someone is and how they relate to her."

Benny Medina, Lopez's manager and business partner of many years and the godfather of her twins, on Lopez's track record as a serial monogamist. March 15, 2012. *Vogue Magazine*

"They are the most traveled two babies besides the Jolie-Pitt children. She got very used to just scooping those kids up and going, whether it was European fashion shows, music-video sets, film locations, *American Idol* judging. She likes to work. The Jennifer DNA is based on work."

Benny Medina on Lopez being a busy mother. March 15, 2012. *Vogue Magazine*

"I had heard rumors that Jennifer was in the loop, and I thought if she did it, I'd do it. She's an alpha female; she's motherly, street, nurturing, and she tells it like it is. When a woman is that strong, she can't be denied. She wasn't shocked by me, and she got me to be more real."

Steven Tyler, lead singer of Aerosmith and fellow judge with Lopez on *American Idol*, on Lopez deciding to do the show. August 4, 2011. *Vanity Fair*

"*Let's Get Loud.*"

Hillary Clinton, US politician, on her favorite Lopez song. October 31, 2016. *Extra*

"Jennifer freaks me out everytime I'm around her. By the time all three of us are muffed and buffed and puffed, I think we're all sexually attracted to each other, first and foremost. There's a lot of healthy adult sexuality going on up there. But what's deeper than that is our music and what we know about music. And Jennifer is such an alpha-female. She comes off as very strong, with a lot of conviction, and very believable. Hence, the American public has fallen in love with her."

Steven Tyler on Lopez and their time together on *American Idol*. March 15, 2012. *Vogue Magazine*

"Jennifer is a very lovely, soulful woman, and she's even more beautiful now than when she was young. She just has such a beautiful persona."

Doug Morris, the C.E.O. of Sony Music, on Lopez. August 4, 2011. *Vanity Fair*

"Jennifer Lopez is like a tall drink of hot cocoa."

Oliver Stone, movie director, on Lopez. February 1, 1998. *Movieline*

"Jennifer Lopez is a perfect example of what it means to be a mogul and have longevity, but still have people like you. She can do this until she chooses not to anymore. I hope I can say that one day."

Naya Rivera, actress, on Lopez. October 25, 2016. *Vivala*

"Jennifer was just wonderful. She was always giving us hugs; she was just someone you could always go to for support."

Scotty McCreery, a past winner of *American Idol*, on Lopez. August 4, 2011. *Vanity Fair*

"Jennifer's really a girly girl, and she loves all aspects of fashion. She's building her brand so that she can cover the woman from head to toe in the JLO style.

The sex is definitely there. She has an affinity for those retro silhouettes, so you'll see baby dolls, onesies - which nobody is really doing - some bustiers, it's all there.

It's really about Jennifer's softer, more feminine side. That plays out in soft pastel colours like pinks, violets, light blues with accents of grey.

Even the everyday stuff is still sexy.

Jennifer likes to hang out at home and watch movies, but she's going to look amazingly sexy while she's doing it. She knows that other women out there want to do the same."

Erin Lynn, marketing director for JLO Lingerie. September 10, 2004. *The Times*

"If you went by what people said . . . I wasn't cool and I wasn't talented. I was, like, the lowest rung of cool and talented that you could possibly be in the public consciousness at that time. I had broken up with Jennifer Lopez and I had, like, three or four movies in a row that had bombed."

Ben Affleck, actor and Lopez's ex-fiancé, on the effect his relationship with Lopez had on his career in the early 2000s. June 27, 2016. *Popsugar*

"I always find any excuse to collaborate with Jennifer... She's my angel. She absolutely is drop-dead gorgeous and powerful and sophisticated and militant and diligent and a hard worker and that is why Jennifer is Jennifer... I learn a lot from her. She's opened a lot of doors for someone such as myself."

Pitbull, a rapper and occasional musical collaborator with Lopez. October 25, 2016. *Vivala*

"The dancers look beautiful, both girls and boys who all looked like her exes! There's lots and lots of booty, and the costumes are those of a fabulous diva. The sets and stage props are super fun, and there was a theme of things appearing out of holes. A hole extravaganza with legs coming out of the wall, trumpets coming out of the floor, and at one point Jennifer dipped her feet into a hole onstage and came back up with a shoe change!"

Emily Jillette, magician Penn Jillette's wife, on Lopez's stage show in Vegas. January 20, 2016. *Las Vegas Sun*

"I don't know why people expect bad things. For some to go through what I did, it would have been easy perhaps to feel hurt and then try to hurt others in turn and insult them. I took another path, the high road. It's all good, I am happy that my kids are loved by everyone."

Dayanara Torres, ex-wife of Marc Anthony (Lopez and Anthony married four days after his divorce from Torres was finalized.) July 16, 2007. *Beyond Beautiful*

"I swear she's my idol, but she is one of the most incredible entertainers of our time."

Adrienne Bailon, talk show host, on Lopez. October 25, 2016. *Vivala*

"To have a superstar like Jennifer Lopez starring in this classic show, which every high school in America has done, will ensure that our holiday musicals continue to be must-see events for the whole family.

It was her idea to take on this classic singing and dancing role made famous by the legendary Chita Rivera, and we are so happy to oblige! This show has delighted audiences for generations with classic songs that include *Put on a Happy Face* and *A Lot of Livin' to Do*, and this will be an extravagant production built around this big star.

She came to us and said 'I love this show, I discovered the music.' She has a big show in Vegas where she does *Lot of Livin'*, which is a song from *Bye Bye Birdie*."

Bob Greenblatt, NBC Entertainment chairman, on Lopez starring and producing in NBC's *Bye Bye Birdie* production. October 28, 2016. *The Brampton Guardian*

"Mariah (Carey) is a legend and is so talented but constantly disses people. It's nasty the way she treats Jennifer [Lopez]."

Demi Lovato, singer, on Mariah Carey's treatment of Lopez. June 17, 2016. *US Weekly*

"Jennifer Lopez is helping change the face of Las Vegas. Where residencies in the past were often loss leaders with casinos counting on people spending money on gambling before and after, the modern-day residency is a huge part of the city's broader appeal away from the blackjack tables.

Where once Las Vegas was seen as a well-lit retirement home for aging, the move now is to younger, more pop-focused artists who want to stay put in one city, live in a nice, big mansion and not schlep around the world on tour."

Michael Cragg, journalist, on Lopez's Vegas residency.
January 20, 2016. *Las Vegas Sun*

"I had never met her. I'd heard she was a fan of mine, and she walked into my dressing room and I said the worst opening line ever. I don't know what the hell came over me, but I said, 'You're my wife and you don't even know it.' And she said, 'Excuse me?' And I'm like, 'I'm so sorry, I don't know where the fuck that came from.' "

Marc Anthony on the day he met Jennifer back in 1998 when Lopez took her father to see Anthony perform on Broadway; he felt from that day that their relationship was destined to be. August 4, 2011. *Vanity Fair*

"Jennifer was always my first choice [for a judge this year]. I just always thought she'd be fantastic on television. And obviously, it all worked out better than anybody probably could have imagined."

Simon Fuller, *American Idol* creator, on Lopez. August 4, 2011. *Vanity Fair*

"I'd be a liar to say that if you have the looks, it doesn't help you. But it doesn't advance you. You have to have something else to back it up. There are tons of beautiful, beautiful people in the world who do all different types of things. Just because you look a certain way doesn't mean you'll be successful in this business."

Adam Shankman, director of *The Wedding Planner*, on not wanting to cast Lopez initially for the movie. January 22, 2001. *The Times-Colonist*

"You can't stop Jennifer's sexuality, but you can definitely curtail it."

Adam Shankman, director of *The Wedding Planner*, on Lopez. January 22, 2001. *The Times-Colonist*

"Lopez has a face so exquisite that it's hard to look directly at it."

Celia Walden, journalist, on Lopez; she interviewed Lopez for a comprehensive article. June 19, 2013. *The Telegraph*

"She's such a strong, confident woman. She's just such an inspirational person and so empowering and if there's anybody that's super radiant and confident, it's her."

Demi Lovato, singer, on Lopez. October 25, 2016. *Vivala*

"I learned so much from her, and she's opened so many doors for people."

Pitbull, a rapper who did a duet with Lopez on *American Idol*, on the performer. August 4, 2011. *Vanity Fair*

"She could enjoy life a little more. I mean, there are only a certain amount of hours in every day. But, we know each other, we know when we can't tolerate each other, and we each have that sounding board [in each other]. She's harsh with her criticism sometimes, but it's just because she wants me to be the best I can be. I will always be there for her. It's a very, very dynamic life. I'm taxing myself and pushing myself to the limit, work-wise. But I've been faced with the phone not ringing, and that's not fun. I'd rather this."

Marc Anthony on whether Lopez works too hard. August 4, 2011. *Vanity Fair*

"I'm not kidding, this woman can really act. The last several years she's been doing romantic comedies - that's a talent, but as a dramatic actress she's got fantastic chops. She knows how to transmit nuances, to make the subtlest of shifts. Does she have humor? Yes. But at the same time she can get into the deepest dramatic areas. I was fascinated and thrilled that she was able to go there.

What I sensed in her is that she is a woman. She's somebody who's reached a certain point of depth. She's a fantastic mother, she cares a lot about her two children, but there's some pain in there. She's had her ups and downs and difficulties in her personal life. But more than anything else I think that whatever the odds are against her, she's never going to give up. I think she's capable of translating that experience into dramatic roles in a way that will surprise a lot of people."

Taylor Hackford, director of *Parker*, which starred Lopez and hit theaters in 2012. March 15, 2012. *Vogue Magazine*

"I admire her in many ways. She is a very powerful woman who has worked her ass off. She has proven herself in so many ways. A singer, actress, business woman, mother, cultural leader to many. She is Jenny from the block but also Jenny that don't stop! She is about her business and is successful at it. She is a strong woman."

Becky G, singer, on Lopez. October 25, 2016. *Vivala*

"Jennifer's uniqueness lies in her combination of extraordinary beauty, intelligence and street smarts. She's a fantastic role model. She *owns* it."

Jane Fonda, fellow actress and co-star of *Monster-in-Law*. October 31, 2011. *Glamour magazine*

"I joke with her that I'm about to pass her — I think I have about 90,000 followers and she has 25 million — but she's obviously very committed to it and very generous with how she communicates with her fans. That's what I'm trying to do as I build this audience."

Harry Connick Jr., a co-host judge on *American Idol*, on what tips Lopez has given him on dealing with Twitter. January 23, 2013. *Adweek*

#####

Hope you've enjoyed this round-up of Lopez's thoughts on her life, her loves, and show business.

Have a great day!

Dream big,

Toby

Printed in Poland
by Amazon Fulfillment
Poland Sp. z o.o., Wrocław

50057111R10045